THE EVOLUTION
OF AFRICA'S MAJOR NATIONS

Algeria

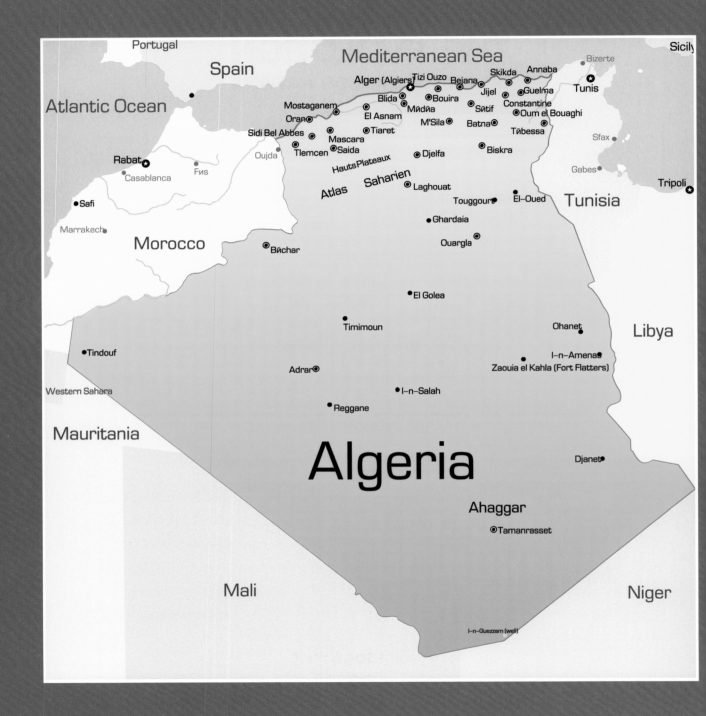

THE EVOLUTION
OF AFRICA'S MAJOR NATIONS

Algeria

Daniel E. Harmon

Mason Crest
Philadelphia

Mason Crest
370 Reed Road
Broomall, PA 19008
www.masoncrest.com

CPSIA Compliance Information: Batch #EAMN2013-3. For further information,
contact Mason Crest at 1-866-MCP-Book.

First printing

1 3 5 7 9 8 6 4 2

Library of Congress Cataloging-in-Publication Data

Harmon, Daniel E.
  Algeria / Daniel E. Harmon.
       p. cm. — (Evolution of Africa's major nations.)
  Includes bibliographical references and index.
  ISBN 978-1-4222-2191-4 (hardcover)
  ISBN 978-1-4222-2219-5 (pbk.)
  ISBN 978-1-4222-9431-4 (ebooks)
  1. Algeria—Juvenile literature. I. Title. II. Series: Evolution of Africa's major nations.
  DT275.H35 2012
  965—dc22
                              2011018505

Table of Contents

Africa: Progress, Problems, and Promise

Robert I. Rotberg

Africa is the cradle of humankind, but for millennia it was off the familiar, beaten path of global commerce and discovery. Its many peoples therefore developed largely apart from the diffusion of modern knowledge and the spread of technological innovation until the 17th through 19th centuries. With the coming to Africa of the book, the wheel, the hoe, and the modern rifle and cannon, foreigners also brought the vastly destructive transatlantic slave trade, oppression, discrimination, and onerous colonial rule. Emerging from that crucible of European rule, Africans created nationalistic movements and then claimed their numerous national independences in the 1960s. The result is the world's largest continental assembly of new countries.

There are 53 members of the African Union, a regional political grouping, and 48 of those nations lie south of the Sahara. Fifteen of them, including mighty Ethiopia, are landlocked, making international trade and economic growth that much more arduous and expensive. Access to navigable rivers is limited, natural harbors are few, soils are poor and thin, several countries largely consist of miles and miles of sand, and tropical diseases have sapped the strength and productivity of innumerable millions. Being landlocked, having few resources (although countries along Africa's west coast have tapped into deep offshore petroleum and gas reservoirs), and being beset by malaria, tuberculosis, schistosomiasis, AIDS, and many other maladies has kept much of Africa poor for centuries.

Thirty-two of the world's poorest 44 countries are African. Hunger is common. So is rapid deforestation and desertification. Unemployment rates are often over 50 percent, for jobs are few—even in agriculture. Where Africa once

Algeria, the second-largest country in Africa, is mostly desert. It has few water sources aside from its border with the Mediterranean.

was a land of small villages and a few large cities, with almost everyone engaged in growing grain or root crops or grazing cattle, camels, sheep, and goats, today more than half of all the more than 1 billion Africans, especially those who live south of the Sahara, reside in towns and cities. Traditional agriculture hardly pays, and a number of countries in Africa—particularly the smaller and more fragile ones—can no longer feed themselves.

There is not one Africa, for the continent is full of contradictions and variety. Of the 750 million people living south of the Sahara, at least 150 million live in Nigeria, 85 million in Ethiopia, 68 million in the Democratic Republic of the Congo, and 49 million in South Africa. By contrast, tiny Djibouti and

A Tuareg man leads camels through the Sahara desert, Algeria.

Equatorial Guinea have fewer than 1 million people each, and prosperous Botswana and Namibia each are under 2.2 million in population. Within some countries, even medium-sized ones like Zambia (12 million), there are a plethora of distinct ethnic groups speaking separate languages. Zambia, typical with its multitude of competing entities, has 70 such peoples, roughly broken down into four language and cultural zones. Three of those languages jostle with English for primacy.

Given the kaleidoscopic quality of African culture and deep-grained poverty, it is no wonder that Africa has developed economically and politically less rapidly than other regions. Since independence from colonial rule, weak governance has also plagued Africa and contributed significantly to the widespread poverty of its peoples. Only Botswana and offshore Mauritius have been governed democratically without interruption since independence. Both are among Africa's wealthiest countries, too, thanks to the steady application of good governance.

Aside from those two nations, and South Africa, Africa has been a continent of coups since 1960, with massive and oil-rich Nigeria suffering incessant periods of harsh, corrupt, autocratic military rule. Nearly every other country on or around the continent, small and large, has been plagued by similar bouts of instability and dictatorial rule. In the 1970s and 1980s Idi Amin ruled Uganda capriciously and Jean-Bedel Bokassa proclaimed himself emperor of the Central African Republic. Macias Nguema of Equatorial Guinea was another in that same mold. More recently Daniel arap Moi held Kenya in thrall and Robert Mugabe has imposed himself on once-prosperous Zimbabwe. In both of those cases, as in the case of Gnassingbe Eyadema in Togo and the late Mobutu Sese Seko in Congo, these presidents stole wildly and drove entire peoples and their nations into penury. Corruption is common in Africa, and so are a weak rule-of-law framework, misplaced development, high expenditures on soldiers and low expenditures on health and education, and a widespread (but not universal) refusal on the part of leaders to work well for their followers and citizens.

Conflict between groups within countries has also been common in Africa. More than 12 million Africans have been killed in civil wars since 1990, while another 9 million have become refugees. Decades of conflict in Sudan led to a January 2011 referendum in which the people of southern Sudan voted overwhelmingly to secede and form a new state. In early 2011, anti-government protests spread throughout North Africa, ultimately toppling long-standing regimes in Tunisia and Egypt. That same year, there were serious ongoing hostilities within Chad, Ivory Coast, Libya, the Niger Delta region of Nigeria, and Somalia.

Despite such dangers, despotism, and decay, Africa is improving. Botswana and Mauritius, now joined by South Africa, Senegal, Kenya, and Ghana, are beacons of democratic growth and enlightened rule. Uganda and Senegal are taking the lead in combating and reducing the spread of AIDS, and others are following. There are serious signs of the kinds of progressive economic policy changes that might lead to prosperity for more of Africa's peoples. The trajectory in Africa is positive.

Most of Algeria is desert and rock. (Opposite) Unusual sandstone formations rise from the Sahara Desert of the Ahaggar Mountains in southern Algeria, west of the town of Tamanghasset. (Right) The Dahar plateau is the westernmost tip of the Atlas Mountain range in Algeria.

The Land

AFRICA IS A HUGE CONTINENT—the second largest on earth, after Asia. Sprawling across its northwestern Sahara region is a big country, the People's Democratic Republic of Algeria. It is the second-largest country in Africa, after Sudan, and is about a third as large as the continental United States.

Although Algeria borders the Mediterranean Sea, it is a land that is seriously poor in water—Algeria has few rivers and freshwater lakes. Most of the country is desert where only a few thousand hardy people live. However, along its northern coastline between the ocean and highlands is a pleasant, long-settled region that has had a strong impact on history. Algeria dominates the southern Mediterranean just inside the Strait of Gibraltar, the Mediterranean's western entrance. This makes Algiers, the nation's capital, a major port of call for vessels sailing between the open Atlantic and the Gulf of Suez at the eastern end of the Mediterranean.

THE MAGHREB—A FERTILE ZONE BETWEEN DESERT AND SEA

The Atlas Mountains sweep across northwestern Africa *parallel* to the Mediterranean shoreline from Tunisia in the east to the Atlantic coast of Morocco in the west. The mountains and the coastal plain leading to the sea are known as the *Maghreb* region of Africa. This stretch of Mediterranean Africa has also been called the Barbary Coast. During the 17th, 18th, and early 19th centuries, sailors dreaded the area because of the notorious "Barbary pirates" who were based there.

At different times in recent history, some of the political leaders of Morocco, Algeria, and Tunisia have sought to form a united Maghreb—or at least establish cooperation among the three neighboring countries. Boundary disputes and other complications have prevented this from happening. Still, the Maghreb binds the inhabitants of northwestern Africa together in important ways. Many researchers who have studied the history, culture, and geology of this part of the world have focused on the Maghreb as a whole, not on any one country.

The northern part of Algeria along the coast, known as the Tell region, has a mild Mediterranean climate with adequate rainfall to support agriculture. Late autumn and winter are its rainy seasons. French settlers who occupied the territory beginning in the 1830s cultivated

THE GEOGRAPHY OF ALGERIA

Location: on the Mediterranean coast of northern Africa between Tunisia and Morocco

Area: (about 3.5 times the size of Texas)
  total: 919,595 square miles (2,381,740 sq km)
  land: 919,595 square miles (2,381,740 sq km)
  water: 0 square miles (0 sq km.)

Borders: Libya 610 miles (982 km); Mali 855 miles (1,376 km); Mauritania 287.7 miles (463 km); Morocco 968.7 miles (1,559 km); Niger 594 miles (956 km); Tunisia 599.6 miles (965 km); Western Sahara 26 miles (42 km)

Climate: arid desert, semiarid coastal zone

Terrain: high plateau and desert across most of the country, few mountains, narrow coastal plain

Elevation extremes:
  lowest point: Chott Melrhir 131 feet (40 m) below sea level
  highest point: Mt. Tahat approximately 9,852 feet (3003 m) above sea level

Natural hazards: earthquakes, flooding and mudslides in the mountains during the rainy season

Source: CIA World Factbook, 2011.

impressive orchards and vineyards. Today, the Tell remains Algeria's farming region. Oaks, pines, and cedars are the most common trees in this area. Brushwood and grass grow on the plateaus. Naturally, it is the part of the country where most people live.

In northeastern Algeria lie two smaller mountain ranges that are separate from the main Atlas chain. The historic city of Constantine is situated in the low-lying Petite Kabyle Mountains near the coast. During the 19th and 20th centuries, French colonists found these highlands especially suitable for growing grains. Located a bit farther south, the Aurès Mountains are rugged

Tourists ride camels on a Mediterranean beach near Algiers.

and forbidding. For centuries Berber rebels and refugees have taken to the Aurès for shelter from invading armies and authorities.

THE SAHARA DESERT

To the south of Algeria's long, east-west mountain ranges, the great Sahara Desert covers a broad swath of northern Africa, from Egypt in the east to Morocco in the west. Most of Algeria is covered by this immense desert.

The name Sahara conjures scenes of vast wind-swept sand dunes. This indeed is a major part of the picture. But the desert also has areas of gravel, rocks, and hills. In the Tassili-n-Ajjer highlands there are strange stone formations—petrified sand dunes—that resemble castles. Not far away, plateaus formed of sandstone are marked by rough gorges—the work of rivers that ran dry thousands of years ago. In other areas, the Sahara is like a pebble-strewn carpet. And at places, especially in the northern half of the desert, there are *oases*, surprising havens of greenery and water amid barren surroundings.

The desert is basically hot and dry. The Sahara receives less than five inches (12.7 centimeters) of rainfall a year. A sandy desert wind called the *sirocco* often blows northward and invades the inhabited areas of the Tell in the summer months. But while the Sahara is lightly populated and harsh, it is vital to Algeria's economy. In the desert of eastern Algeria lies much of the country's mineral wealth, including natural gas and petroleum. Today, a north-south highway through the Sahara Desert connects Algiers with Lagos, the largest city in Nigeria, far to the south.

ALGERIAN WILDLIFE

The only bird found exclusively in Algeria is the Algerian nuthatch. It is a small songbird with the big head, short tail, and powerful beak that are characteristic of all nuthatches. Only discovered in 1973, the Algerian nuthatch lives in four areas of mountain forest in the northeastern part of the country. Additionally, it only lives in places above an elevation of 3,300 feet. The Algerian nuthatch is blue-grey with a buff-colored belly. The male has a black crown and eyestripe, while the female has a grey crown and eyestripe. There are less than 4,000 of these birds in existence, so they are listed as officially endangered. Logging and fires are the greatest threats to their habitat.

Another endangered bird of the Maghreb is the waldrapp, or northern bald ibis. This bird has black, glossy feathers, a bald, red head, and a red

The northern bald ibis is nearly extinct.

bill. It makes its home in the rocky desert where it feeds on insects and rodents. There are estimated to be 420 waldrapps left in the wild. Their decline is linked to loss of habitat, hunting, and poisoning from pesticides. Conservation groups have been breeding the birds in captivity in the hopes of being able to reintroduce some into the wild. Although they are now only found in the Moroccan portion of the Maghreb, their range used to cover all of North Africa.

Also unique to the Maghreb are Barbary macaques. Sometimes called Barbary apes, these primates are actually monkeys. They inhabit the oak and cedar forests in the north of Algeria, and a small band lives in Gibraltar, making them the only primates in Europe other than humans. The macaques have long fur that ranges in color from yellow-grey to grey-brown. They have dark colored faces and no tails. Macaques are mostly herbivores, eating leaves, roots, and fruit, but they will also eat insects.

Barbary macaques live in mixed-gender groups of 10 to 30 members headed by the dominant female. Male Barbary macaques are active participants in raising the young. They will play with them and groom them, which is a unique behavior among macaque species. When choosing mates, female macaques seem to prefer those males with good parental skills. Barbary macaques bear one offspring per mating season; twins are very uncommon. Due to logging and local farmers, the macaques in the Maghreb are endangered. Although the Moroccan macaque population ranges from 6,000-10,000, there are only 1,200-2,000 left in Algeria, and another 200-300 in Gibraltar.

Another inhabitant of Algeria is the sand cat. These creatures live in the sand dunes of the Sahara, and their tan coats blend well into that environment. They have a broad head with large close-set eyes. Their ears are large to make it easier to find scarce prey. The dunes muffle sound quite well, so the sand cat needs extra sensitive hearing in order to find food. Another one of their desert adaptations is the long hairs which cover the pads of their

Barbary macaques are very social animals that split their time between living in trees and living on the ground.

feet. These create cushions, which insulate them from the hot sand. They also make it easier to move silently over the loose terrain.

Sand cats are expert diggers. They dig burrows to live in and dig rodents out of the sand for food. Because of this, their claws are not particularly sharp. Sand cats will eat whatever they can find, such as gerbils, sand voles, reptiles, and insects. These cats are also known to be particularly adept snake hunters. They will stun a snake with rapid blows to the head before biting its neck for the kill.

It is believed that the cat originally domesticated by the Egyptians was a sand cat. Given their ability to hunt rodents and kill snakes, these small cats would have been a blessing to any town they wandered near. It is thought that grateful humans began to leave food out for the cats as a way to thank them for taking care of pests.

Among the pests that the sand cats would have hunted is the sand viper. These pale snakes have three rows of brown spots that run the length of their bodies. They bury themselves in the sand during the day and emerge at night to eat. Sand vipers are cantankerous and quick to strike. Their venom is hemotoxic. This means that it destroys red blood cells, keeps blood from clotting, and destroys organs. Permanent damage is common, even if antivenom is applied quickly.

NOT ALWAYS DESERT

Scientists believe that in prehistoric times the Sahara was not the desert it is today but was instead a fertile, grassy region called a *savanna*. Cave art discovered in the southeastern mountains of Ahaggar in Tassili-n-Ajjer, estimated to be as old as 8,000 years, tells of a people that once thrived in what now is the hot, dry Sahara. Scientists believe that the people who made these paintings were hunters of the Neolithic Age. At the time, the region was alive with the kinds of animals that still are common to other parts of Africa, such as rhinoceroses, elephants, hippopotamuses, lions, and buffalos.

Today, of course, that is quite changed. The bleak plateaus of the Ahaggar Highlands have been compared to the surface of the moon. Even in the region north of the Atlas Mountains, forestland has been lost to the spread of civilization in recent generations.

Algeria, to most foreigners, is simply one of several vast countries devoured by the Sahara, appealing to few but the most adventurous outsiders. However, it is unique among its neighbors. Its particular combination of people, cultures, politics, problems, and historical development is found in no other country.

People have fought for control of Algeria for a long time. (Opposite) Algerians celebrate their hard-won independence from France, 1962. (Right) Roman ruins at Tipasa. The Romans fought three wars with the powerful North African city-state of Carthage. In 146 B.C., Rome finally destroyed Carthage and gained control of the Algeria region.

2 Algeria's History

THE FERTILE COASTAL PLAIN of what is now Algeria has been inhabited and controlled by many different peoples. The indigenous inhabitants of North Africa are collectively known as the Berbers, tribes of nomads whose origin is not clearly understood. Their society was not highly organized, making them vulnerable to outsiders.

About 4,000 years ago, the seafaring Phoenicians began to establish coastal trading settlements along the coast of North Africa. One of the most important Phoenician cities was Carthage, in modern-day Tunisia. The city was founded in the ninth century B.C. and eventually became a wealthy trading center and a powerful military kingdom. By the sixth century B.C. other Phoenician colonies of North Africa were under its influence. In a series of struggles for control of the Mediterranean world, Carthage found itself repeatedly at war. It fought the Greeks in the fourth century B.C. In the third and second centuries B.C., it conducted a series of lengthy campaigns against the city-state of Rome, known as the Punic Wars.

During the Punic Wars, much of the area of modern-day Algeria was called Numidia. Not all the city kings in Numidia supported Carthage. One Numidian king, Masinissa, helped the Romans win a decisive battle over the Cathaginians in 202 B.C. The Romans rewarded Masinissa by giving him authority over all Numidia. He made his capital at Cirta, which today is the city of Constantine.

Between 149 and 146 B.C. Roman forces destroyed Carthage. Eventually, Rome took over Numidia and other parts of North Africa as well. The Roman Empire ruled northern Africa for more than 500 years. However, the empire gradually weakened and was eventually overrun by barbarian forces. In A.D. 429, a tribe of people called the Vandals crossed into northern Africa from Spain. The Vandals captured Carthage, ending Roman control in this part of the Maghreb.

THE COMING OF THE ARABS

During the seventh and eighth centuries A.D., Arabs from the Middle East invaded and conquered the Berber lands of northwestern Africa. Although the inhabitants resisted, over time the Arab Muslims and Berbers intermarried and blended their customs and traditions. The Islamic religion and the Arabic language became dominant.

Europeans came to call these inhabitants of North Africa the Moors. During the eighth century the Moors crossed the Mediterranean and invaded the Iberian Peninsula, conquering modern-day Spain and Portugal and establishing an Islamic kingdom there. Moorish cities like Andalusia, Toledo, and Granada became centers for learning and culture in Medieval Europe. But between the 11th and 15th centuries, European Christians living in what today is Spain began a gradual reconquest of the European territory, and the Moors retreated to North Africa.

Soon after the last of the Moors left Spain in 1492, the Ottoman Turks began invading and conquering the Maghreb. The Turks built an empire throughout the Middle East and North Africa from their power base in what is today Turkey. The Berbers could not hold them back, for they had no unified government or army. The Berbers had only wandering tribes (some stronger than others) and a variety of villages (some larger than others). However, some Berber *corsairs* tried to resist the Ottomans and also fight the Spanish Christians from their coastal strongholds. Spanish commerce, in particular, suffered at the hands of the corsairs, so Spain established a fort at Peñon, an island in the Bay of Algiers.

The angry *emir*, or ruler, of Algiers pleaded with the corsairs to oust the Europeans from Peñon. Kheir-ed-din Barbarossa and his brother Arouj responded by assassinating the emir and installing themselves as rulers. Arouj was killed in a battle with the Spaniards in 1518. But in 1529 Barbarossa drove the Spaniards from Peñon. He then claimed the territory for the Ottoman Empire and was made an admiral in their fleet. He made Algiers a base for the notorious Barbary pirates of the lower Mediterranean coast. The Turks and their pirate allies would dominate the Maghreb for the next three centuries.

Wealthy Ottomans supported the Barbary corsairs, supplying them with ships. In return, the backers received a percentage of the goods and treasures the pirates captured at sea. Over the years, the corsairs took tens of thousands of prisoners, holding them in horrible conditions and forcing governments and families to pay money to have them freed. The leaders of the Barbary States (Algeria, Tripoli, Morocco, and Tunisia) demanded **tributes** from foreign governments to ensure safe passage for their ships.

The raids of the Barbary pirates led to conflicts with many European governments and, during the early 1800s, with the newly independent United States. But it would fall to the French to finally end the Barbary pirates' dreaded reign in northern Africa. In 1827 France dispatched forces to Algiers to blockade the port and stop the Barbary pirates.

THE FRENCH ERA

During the 19th century European nations began jockeying for control over the African continent. In 1830 France officially declared Algeria its territory.

To lure colonists to Algeria, the French government made an attractive offer: it would give European emigrants to Algeria free land, livestock, and seeds for planting crops. It would even ship them across the Mediterranean to their new homes at no cost. The strategy was effective. By 1875 almost 300,000 Europeans were living in Algeria—approximately one-tenth of the country's population. By 1911 the Europeans numbered 752,000.

Europeans in Algeria during the colonial period were known as **colons** or **pieds-noirs** ("black feet"—a name probably given to them because French soldiers wore black shoes). Algerian natives were called *indigènes*. Although

France controlled the country, an estimated 80 percent of Europeans living in Algeria by the 1900s were from other countries, particularly Spain and Italy. In certain towns and neighborhoods, more residents spoke Spanish than French.

The Europeans took over the best farmland, displacing native Algerians. *Indigènes* were taxed heavily but received few benefits from the colonial government in return. The French colonial administration required Muslims in Algeria to carry passes and obtain government permission before they were allowed to travel.

A BLOODY ROAD TO INDEPENDENCE

The unfair practices and policies of the French rulers of Algeria led to various uprisings and independence movements. Indigène uprisings began as early as 1871 but were put down harshly by the French. Discontent grew more intense as the growing Muslim population fell deeper and deeper into

French colonial officials distribute food to the Arab population in Setif. This illustration was originally published in a Paris magazine in 1868.

poverty. Deprived of good farmland and unable to get factory jobs, they seethed at their French overlords. After the end of World War II in 1945, the movement for Algerian independence gained strength, breaking into a bloody rebellion in 1954.

By 1960 an estimated 300,000 French soldiers, joined by 150,000 Muslim volunteers, were at war against an estimated 50,000 guerrilla fighters of the Front de Libération Nationale (FLN). The FLN was a Muslim organization determined to drive out the French. The colonial administration's soldiers were more numerous and better armed, so FLN guerrillas resorted to terrorist attacks against civilians. They ambushed buses and concealed time bombs in restaurants and stores, for example. It was a brutal way to fight the war for independence—especially since FLN attacks killed nine times as many Algerian Muslims as French soldiers. In the end, it is estimated that a million Algerians—one-tenth of the population—died as a result of the eight-year struggle.

French Foreign Legion soldiers search an Algerian civilian in 1962, during a time of unrest.

As the war dragged on, the French found themselves in an impossible situation. The French government tried in vain to win the allegiance of poor Muslim villagers by improving their living conditions. Soldiers constructed huts and water systems and provided basic supplies. Volunteer nurses and teachers from France went out to remote mountain villages to help. The rebels responded by destroying the new *utility* works, putting land mines on railroad tracks, and ambushing buses and relief convoys. French soldiers had to accompany travelers while fighter planes scouted the road ahead to look for signs of guerrilla units.

The people of France eventually forced the government to end its increasingly unpopular fight to keep control of Algeria. In 1962 the French military withdrew from Algeria, and many Europeans fled the country. Revolutionaries executed other Algerians suspected of supporting the French. It was a frightful time. Arab-Berbers and Europeans alike wondered what would become of Algeria.

INDEPENDENT ALGERIA

Ahmad Ben Bella, a leader of the militant revolutionaries, emerged as independent Algeria's first premier. By having rival leaders arrested or forced into exile, Ben Bella set himself up as Algeria's undisputed ruler. However, he was brought down just three years later in a bloodless coup led by a trusted military commander, Colonel Houari Boumédiènne. Boumédiènne then served as president of Algeria until his death in 1978. Boumédiènne had instituted *socialist* reforms in Algeria, redistributing farmland to peasants. Under his rule, the country was largely controlled by the military. Boumédiènne was succeeded by another army officer, Colonel Chadli Bendjedid.

Independence brought an end to the long, bloody revolution, but it did not bring an end to unrest in Algeria. The FLN was the only political party allowed to participate in Algeria's government, and this angered some people. In 1988, after a series of violent protests, President Bendjedid permitted changes to Algeria's constitution that allowed new political parties to form.

In 1990 and 1991, a party called the Front Islamique du Salut (Islamic Salvation Front, or FIS) received strong support in local and national elections. Leaders of the FIS were Islamic fundamentalists, or *Islamists.* One of their goals was to make Islamic religious laws and teachings the basis for Algeria's government.

Leaders of the military were afraid the FIS would gain control of the National Assembly, which could enable the party to carry out its plan to make Algeria a *theocracy*. To prevent this from happening, the military forced Bendjedid to resign and canceled elections for the Assembly that had been scheduled for 1992. The new military-backed government declared a state of emergency in Algeria, giving it authority to sharply curtail people's freedom in the name of national security.

CIVIL WAR IN ALGERIA

The cancellation of the election sparked a civil war. Members of the FIS formed a resistance force, the Islamic Salvation Army. Two other guerilla groups—the Armed Islamic Group (GIA) and Islamic Armed Movement (MIA)—also formed at this time. The GIA was based in towns while the MIA fought in the outlying mountain regions. They initially focused their attacks on the army and military installations, but soon moved on to attacking civilian targets.

In 1994 the Algerian government made some progress in negotiating with the FIS, but this angered the GIA. The MIA joined the FIS to form the Islamic Salvation Army (AIS), and both went to war against the GIA, which soon began a campaign targeting entire villages.

The first of the three sides to give in was the Islamic Salvation Army, which asked the government for a ceasefire in 1997. The GIA eventually fell apart over internal disagreements about its policy of

A mosque in Algiers, capital of Algeria. During the early 1990s, Islamic fundamentalists appeared poised to take control of Algeria's government. The Algerian military stepped in to prevent this, touching off a bloody civil war.

massacring civilians. After Algeria held elections in 1999, newly elected president Abdelaziz Bouteflika's government granted *amnesty* to the militants who had not committed serious crimes. The Islamic Salvation Army was dissolved, although remnants of the GIA continued to be a problem into the new century. Overall, more than 150,000 Algerians are believed to have been killed during the civil war.

Terrorism remains a considerable threat in Algeria, but instances of large-scale violence are much less common. One group still actively fighting is the Salafist Group for Preaching and Combat (GSPC), an organization that broke away from the GIA in 1998. In January 2007 the group changed its name to the Al-Qaeda Organization in the Islamic Maghreb, reflecting its links to the international terrorist organization founded by Osama bin Laden. This group launched numerous attacks throughout 2007 and 2008, including the car-bombing of a UN building that killed dozens of people. In April, 2010, Algeria, Mauritania, Mali, and Nigeria responded by officially joining forces to combat terrorism.

ARAB SPRING PROTESTS

Seventeen people were killed by an al-Qaeda bomb that exploded at this United Nations facility in Algiers, December 2007.

On December 18, 2010, in neighboring Tunisia a fruit vendor named Mohamed Bouazizi committed suicide by lighting himself on fire to protest police corruption and bad treatment. This incident touched off a wave of protests against the Tunisian government, which forced the Tunisian president, Zine El Abidine Ben Ali, to flee the country in mid-January.

Protests soon erupted in other Arab countries, include Algeria, where the first demonstrations occurred on December 28, 2010. The Algerian protestors were angry about high unemployment, particularly among young people, as well as high food prices, government corruption, and restrictions on freedom. The Algerians generally used civil disobedience techniques, mounting sustained campaigns involving strikes, demonstrations, marches, and rallies. In some cases, though, protestors threw stones or Molotov cocktails at Algerian police attempting to disperse the demonstrators. As in other countries, events were often coordinated through social media sites such as Facebook and Twitter.

Police in riot gear arrive at an anti-government demonstration in Algiers, January 2011.

The Bouteflika government attempted to suppress the protests, sometimes through violent means, but this proved impossible. In February, due to continuing public pressure, the government lifted the 19-year-old state of emergency decree, ending many restrictions. On April 15, President Bouteflika spoke on Algerian television, promising to seek constitutional amendments that would provide greater democracy and broader freedom for the media and for political parties. Despite these assurances, protests against the government continued to occur in Algeria.

In recent years the people of Algeria have gained greater opportunities to participate in politics. (Opposite) A woman casts her vote in a 2005 referendum. (Right) Algerian Prime Minister Ahmed Ouyahia meets with U.S. Secretary of Defense Donald Rumsfeld in February 2006. The two countries have agreed to cooperate in efforts to combat terrorism.

3 Government and Foreign Relations

AFTER GAINING INDEPENDENCE, Algeria established a socialist state under the Ahmad Ben Bella administration. The socialist form of government is patterned after that of the Soviet Union. In the Soviet Union the government took control over all industry in the hopes of raising efficiency in all sectors. Farms were seized from those who owned them and changed into collective farms. Collective farms were larger than individual farms and could therefore be worked using modern tractors instead of horses and plows. The goal was to increase food production and thereby raise the economic prospects of the entire country.

Originally, socialism seemed necessary for the new Algeria. After French businesspeople and public officials departed the country, factories were left deserted and unemployment soared. The government hoped its intervention could stabilize the economy. However, socialism was not a tremendous success in Algeria. Agriculture, for example, was less productive because the cooperative farms had inefficient and incompetant management. The country was not raised out of its economic depression like its leaders had hoped. To fight poverty the Algerian market has since moved toward a Western-style setup with the privatization of many formerly government-owned industries.

The FLN was Algeria's only political party during the first decades of independence. A November 1988 amendment to the constitution enabled Algeria to become a multi-party democracy and ended the commitment to socialism. The Ministry of the Interior officially approves all new political parties; to date, there have been more than 40.

THE EXECUTIVE BRANCH

Presidential elections are held every five years, and all citizens aged 18 and over are eligible to vote. Once elected the president appoints a prime minister who then appoints a cabinet of other officials to oversee different areas of government. The president is responsible for national defense and dealing with foreign policy. He is the commander of the armed forces and appoints his generals. The president also appoints the president of the State Council, the magistrates, the governor of the Central Bank, and provincial governors. The president has the right to decree laws in a state of emergency or state of war.

The current president of Algeria is Abdelaziz Bouteflika. He was elected in 1999, having been the preferred candidate of the Algerian military. He was also the only candidate, as complaints about fraud caused all other candidates to withdraw from the election in protest. While Bouteflika's first election was

Algerian president Abdelaziz Bouteflika is currently serving his third term as president.

under dubious circumstances, his reelection in 2004 was hailed as a model for the democratic process. Bouteflika's economic policies in his first term were successful enough to earn him reelection against five other opponents.

Although Algeria's constitution originally limited the president to two five-year terms, in 2008 the constitution was amended to allow unlimited terms. Bouteflika was elected easily to a third term in 2009, receiving over 90 percent of the vote. However, this time international observers of the electoral process in Algeria noted that the election was not fairly contested. The Bouteflika government largely controlled the election process, including which candidates would run in opposition. As a result, many Algerians declined to participate in the elections, believing them to be a sham. Although official figures said that more than 74 percent of Algerians voted, other sources found that the voter participation level might have been as low as 16 percent.

THE LEGISLATIVE BRANCH

Just like the United States Congress, Algeria's legislature is divided into an upper and a lower house. The lower house is the National People's Assembly, consisting of 389 representatives who are elected to five-year terms. The legislature meets for two sessions a year, each lasting at least four months. In 2012, only an estimated 30 percent of eligible voters cast ballots in the election for the National People's Assembly election, suggesting that a large number of Algerians feel disillusioned when it comes to politics.

The upper legislative body, the Council of Nations, consists of 144 members. Two-thirds of them are elected; the others are appointed by the president. Council members serve six-year terms in office. For purposes of local administration, Algeria is divided into 48 provinces, called *wilayas*, governed by regional officials. The current arrangement of *wilayas* has not changed since 1983, although the divisions have been altered more than once since independence.

The legislature passes laws pertaining to rights and duties of individuals, personal status and family law, nationality and immigration, the judicial branch and its jurisdiction, criminal law, finance, public health, labor, defense, and international relations. The People's Assembly approves laws by majority, while the Council of Nations must approve by a three-fourths vote.

Mourad Medelci has served as Algeria's foreign minister since 2007.

THE JUDICIAL BRANCH

The Supreme Judicial Council oversees the nomination of judges and functioning of the courts. The first level courts are called *daira*. These courts are presided over by a single judge. Civil, commercial, and minor criminal cases are heard in this lowest level tribunal.

Above the *daira* are provincial courts. Three judges preside over these mid-level courts, which are split into civil, criminal, administrative, and accusation. Appeals from the *daira* are heard in provincial (*wilaya*) courts.

The Supreme Court has a chamber for private law, covering civil and commercial cases; social law, hearing social security and labor cases; criminal law; and administration. In the cities of Oran, Constantine, and Algiers, there are courts that deal with economic crimes against the state.

The Constitutional Council, established in 1989, determines the constitutionality of law, much like the Supreme Court of the United States.

INTERNATIONAL RELATIONS

Since independence, Algerian leaders have been wary of forming close alliances with other countries. During the Cold War, for example, Algeria was among the leaders of the Non-Aligned Movement, a group of countries that refused to side with either the United States or the Soviet Union. However, Algeria has joined several organizations that reflect the country's support of Arab and African unity. In 1989 Algerian leaders helped form the Union of the Arab Maghreb, a group of northwest African coastal nations seeking to improve economic and trade policies in the region. Algeria is also a member of the Organization of Petroleum Exporting Countries (OPEC), a coalition of mostly Arab nations with significant oil resources; the Arab League, an organization that includes all of the countries in the Arab world; the African Union, a group interested in promoting economic success in Africa and unity among African nations; and the Organization of the Islamic Conference, designed to improve international relations between predominantly Muslim states. When neighboring North African nations Ethiopia and Eritrea attempted to settle a vicious border dispute, Algeria worked with other countries to aid the 2000 peace process.

The relationship between the United States and Algeria was shaky for many years. In 1962, when Algeria became independent, the U.S. was not only allied with France but was also in the midst of the Cold War. American leaders were not sure what to make of the socialist Algerian government. However, the situation has changed. In July 2001 President Bouteflika visited the White House, the first Algerian president to do so in 15 years. In recent years Algeria and the United States have agreed to work together to fight international terrorism.

Historically, Algeria has supported the Palestine Liberation Organization in its long dispute with Israel over control of territory in the Jordan River region. However, in recent years, Algerian leaders have expressed hope for a peaceful solution to the Israeli-Palestinian conflict.

Algeria is on fairly stable terms with most of its geographic neighbors, with the notable exception of Morocco. It violently disputed its northwestern boundary with Morocco after independence. After years of combat and tension, the two countries agreed in 1972 on a borderline of almost a thousand

View of a camp for Saharawi refugees from the Western Sahara, established near Tindouf in the mid-1970s. It is estimated that approximately 90,000 Sahrawi refugees are currently living in one of several camps in Algeria while the dispute over Western Sahara remains unsettled.

miles. But three years later, tensions led to the closing of part of the border, a situation that lasted until 1983. Conflict also arose in 1976 when the Sahrawi Polisario Front, a rebel group in the Moroccan Western Sahara territory, began fighting Morocco for independence. The Moroccan government was not pleased when Algeria announced its support of the Polisario independence movement. Although interaction between Morocco and Algeria remains icy, with each country accusing the other of harboring militant activity and smuggling arms, a positive development occurred in 2004 when Morocco lifted visa requirements on Algerian citizens.

Just as illegal aliens from poorer countries enter the United States, illegal aliens from the Maghreb have sought better lives in Europe. An estimated 5 million people of Algerian descent live in France today, and there are significant Algerian immigrant populations in Spain, Italy, and Germany as well.

Two of Algeria's most important industries are oil and agriculture. (Opposite) These oil pipes carry Algeria's most valuable asset, oil, to a refinery. Oil generates approximately $50 billion a year for Algeria. (Right) Algerian farmers cultivate a patch of peas in the Saida region, 200 miles (322 km) southwest of Algiers.

4 The Economy

WHEN ALGERIA GAINED ITS INDEPENDENCE in 1962, the native Arab-Berber population did not suddenly become prosperous. Algeria's economy was in bad shape after eight years of civil war, and when the French withdrew, some 800,000 European residents fled the country. Since they included most of the skilled labor force as well as doctors, teachers, experienced administrators, and other professionals, Algeria was left in disarray. Factories were shut down. Farms could produce little. For a while more than two-thirds of the new nation's population were out of work.

In the 1970s the country began to recover thanks to valuable resources that had lain hidden in the ground beneath Algeria: oil, natural gas, and minerals.

THE ECONOMY OF ALGERIA

Gross domestic product (GDP*):
$251.1 billion
Inflation: 5%
Natural resources: primarily petroleum, natural gas, iron, uranium, lead, phosphates, zinc
Agriculture (8.3% of GDP): wheat, oats, barley, olives, grapes, citrus fruits, livestock (sheep, cattle)
Industry (61.5% of GDP): petroleum, natural gas, light industries, mining, electrical, petrochemical, food processing
Services (30.2% of GDP): government, tourism, banking, other

Foreign trade:
Exports–$52.66 billion: oil and petroleum products, natural gas
Imports–$37.07 billion: capital goods, foodstuffs, consumer goods
Economic growth rate: 3.3%
Currency exchange rate: U.S. $1 = 72.08 Algerian dinars (2011)

*GDP is the total value of goods and services produced in a country annually.
All figures are 2010 estimates unless otherwise indicated.
Source: CIA World Factbook, 2011.

ALGERIA'S IMPORTANT NATURAL RESOURCES

Fuel sources, or **hydrocarbons**, are Algeria's most valuable economic assets. Sales of natural gas and oil to world markets have made Algeria fairly prosperous compared to other African countries. They account for more than half of the country's national income.

Oil was discovered in the Algerian desert in 1956 and began to be *exported* five years later. Algeria's estimated oil reserves make it the world's 16th most oil-rich nation. Natural gas is an important asset as well, as Algeria has the tenth-largest gas reserve in the world.

Other mineral exports are less significant but make an important contribution to Algeria's economy. These include iron ore, phosphates, zinc, and mercury.

Agriculture is a less lucrative part of the nation's economy, in part because farming is limited by the desert terrain and confined to the northernmost part of the country. Less than 4 percent of the land in Algeria can be farmed. On it, Algerians grow barley, wheat, and other grains; citrus, grapes, and other fruits; and a variety of vegetables. They raise cows, sheep, and other livestock, but have to *import* much of their animal feed from other countries.

On the coast fishermen take their living from the ageless Mediterranean. Algeria's fishing industry is not well developed, however. Overall, the country's farm and fishing production is not enough to meet everyone's food needs, so the government is forced to import other edibles from abroad.

What little farmland exists has been abused. Since Algeria has so little grazing land, livestock owners tend to overgraze the pastures. This results in soil erosion, which makes the land less able to produce in the next growing season. Another form of damage caused by unsound farming practices is the polluting run-off of fertilizer from fields and orchards. It drains into streams, rivers, and ultimately the Mediterranean Sea. This has threatened Algeria's delicate supply of adequate drinking water for its people.

LIVING STANDARDS

In many ways Algerians are better off than many people in other parts of Africa and the Middle East. They receive a free education and basic medical

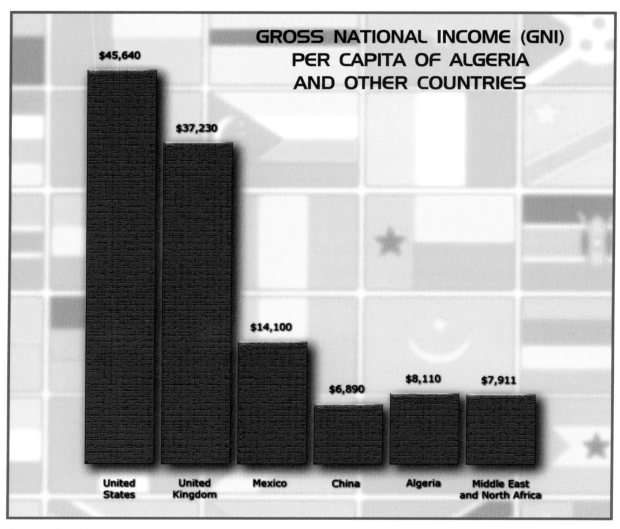

GROSS NATIONAL INCOME (GNI) PER CAPITA OF ALGERIA AND OTHER COUNTRIES

Country	GNI per capita
United States	$45,640
United Kingdom	$37,230
Mexico	$14,100
China	$6,890
Algeria	$8,110
Middle East and North Africa	$7,911

Gross national income per capita is the total value of all goods and services produced domestically in a year, supplemented by income received from abroad, divided by midyear population. The above figures take into account fluctuations in currency exchange rates and differences in inflation rates across global economies, so that an international dollar has the same purchasing power as a U.S. dollar has in the United States.   Source: World Bank, 2011.

care. But many Algerians also live in poverty and struggle to endure the hardships caused by unemployment and inadequate housing.

Housing has been a problem in the country since independence. When the Europeans left, their empty houses were taken over by squatters. And while this provided shelter to some Algerians moving to the city, it was not enough. The Algerian government halted all new construction in the cities to try to stem the tide of migrants, but this simply resulted in shantytowns called *bidonvilles* and some of the highest occupancy rates in the world (an average of 7.5 people per house). Algeria is currently short 1.5 million houses, even after massive construction projects throughout the 1990s. To combat this, in 2006 the government announced plans to build 1 million new units with the help of UN-HABITAT, a UN initiative to reduce slums around the world and replace them with sustainable housing.

INFRASTRUCTURE

While many American households have more than one telephone line, in Algeria there is one telephone for every 20 people, on average. There is one radio for perhaps every four people—and fewer than half as many television sets. In 2007 it was estimated that less than 2 million people out of a population of more than 32 million were Internet users.

While technologically poor, Algeria is fairly well connected when it comes to transportation. Several major east-west highways run through northern Algeria between the Moroccan and Tunisian borders, as does a rail line. Shorter roads connect towns and cities, and the larger cities are linked by rail, as well. More primitive roadways extend through the desert toward the neighboring countries to the south. In all, about 67,300 miles (108,300 km) of highways crisscross the country. About two-thirds of the roads are paved; the rest are gravel or simply packed earth.

The country has approximately 2,470 miles (3,973 km) of railroads, used mainly for transporting cargo. And it has more than 140 airports and airstrips, although fewer than half of them have paved tarmacs. International airports serve Algiers and several other large cities.

PROSPERITY AND PROBLEMS

As a nation, Algeria has fared better than most African states that became independent during the mid-20th century. It earns almost twice as much money selling fuel and other products to foreign countries as it spends buying food and other goods from abroad. Algeria faces difficult economic challenges, however. Most disturbing is its dependence on petroleum and natural gas for so much of its national income. Oil and gas reserves cannot last forever; in time they will be gone. And even while they exist, their prices rise and fall as a result of worldwide factors beyond Algeria's control. When the price of raw fuels goes up, fuel-producing nations such as Algeria reap heady profits on the global market. When they drop, the government must tighten its budget, which can be difficult.

The country also suffers from high unemployment. As of 2011 Algeria's labor force was about 9.9 million workers; according to official government figures, one out of 10 Algerians is unemployed. The government may be understating the unemployment figures, however, as it is particularly hard for young Algerians to find jobs. According to some experts, the unemployment rate

A woman begs for a handout on a street in Algiers. According to official statistics, about 10 percent of working-age Algerians cannot find jobs. However, the real unemployment figure may be much higher. As a result, a high percentage of Algeria's population lives in poverty.

among Algerians under the age of 30 may be as high as 75 percent—one of the key issues fueling the anti-government protests that broke out in January 2011 and continued regularly throughout that year. The nation's leaders recognize the need to find new ways to support the oil-based economy, but this is no easy task in a land that is mostly desert.

Almost all Algerians are Muslim, but there are significant ethnic differences within the population. (Opposite) Berbers celebrate a day of ethnic unity. They make up about 20 percent of the population and are mainly distinguished by the language they speak. (Right) Bedouin women near Touggourt are pictured in front of their tent.

5 Culture and People

THE PEOPLE OF ALGERIA and other Maghreb countries are predominantly a mixture of Arabs and Berbers. Arabs began migrating across northern Africa during the mid-600s. They dominated the territory and intermarried with the native Berbers. It has been estimated that about 80 percent of Algerians today are Arabs, while 20 percent are Berbers. However, it can be a difficult task to distinguish between "Arabs" and "Berbers" when discussing the people of Algeria. (Since the 1960s, the government census has not specified Berbers as a separate category of the population.) Many Algerians who consider themselves Arabs have both Arab and Berber ancestors.

Berbers and Arabs still clash over issues of cultural identity, language, and representation in the government. Since Arabs and Berbers are often racially indistinguishable, they have come to identify themselves based on the language they speak. The Berber language, Tamazight, is not an official language in Algeria, despite being spoken by 15 to 30 percent of the population. The Arabization of Algeria has left the Berbers a marginalized people who do not feel that their culture is respected or represented in their own country. The government even went so far as to create of list of approved names for children—a list that did not contain popular Berber names.

Despite both groups following Islam, Berbers feel that some Muslim leaders consider them insufficiently Muslim because they do not speak Arabic. This tension will sometimes break out in rioting, but by and large, Algeria has been relatively free of the kind of ethnic violence that has been catastrophic in other African nations. Arab-Berber skirmishes and riots are on a much smaller scale than the kind of ethnic violence seen elsewhere.

Berbers have tried to use diplomacy, rather than violence, to solve their problems. And in 2002 the government finally made a concession to their demands, declaring Tamazight a national language, though not an official language. It was a step that many were happy to see, although it does not solve the tension.

THE BERBERS: ALGERIA'S ORIGINAL INHABITANTS

The term "Berber" comes from the Latin word *barbara*—"barbarians." But Berbers inhabited northern Africa many centuries before the Roman period. Early Berbers had a diverse culture with physical differences among the tribes. Today, after many centuries of contact and intermarriage with various peoples who conquered and settled the region, the most common characteristic of Berbers is their language.

THE PEOPLE OF ALGERIA

Population: 34,994,937 (July 2011 est.)
Ethnic groups: Arab-Berber 99%,
   European less than 1%
Age structure:
   0–14 years: 24.2%
   15–64 years: 70.6%
   65 years and over: 5.2%
Birth rate: 16.69/1,000 population
Infant mortality rate: 25.81
   deaths/1,000 live births
Death rate: 4.69 deaths/1,000 people
Population growth rate: 1.173%
Life expectancy at birth:
   total population: 74.5 years

   male: 72.78 years
   female: 76.31 years
Total fertility rate: 1.75 children
   born/woman
Religions: Sunni Muslim 99%, Christian
   and Jewish 1%
Languages: Arabic (official language),
   French, Berber dialects
Literacy: 69.9% (2002 est.)

All figures are 2011 estimates unless otherwise
   indicated.
Source: Adapted from CIA World Factbook, 2011.

Apart from the dominant Arab-Berber population, four major, separate groups of Berbers in Algeria are descended from the early inhabitants. Each group speaks a dialect of its own. The largest group of Berbers in Algeria is the Kabyles, who live atop the mountains near the coastline east of Algiers. Historically regarded as clannish and independent-minded, the Kabyles follow the authority of their own village councils, called *jamaa*. Kabyles are famous in Algerian history for their series of revolts against the French administration during the late 1800s. Today, the *jamaa* continue to be a source for leadership even though the Algerian government has established civil administrations.

The Chaouia inhabit the Aurès Mountains in eastern Algeria. Where possible, Chaouia grow grain and cultivate orchards. In less farmable areas, they herd livestock from pasture to pasture, following the seasons in a quest for adequate grazing.

Nomadic Tuareg Berbers, also known as the blue people, live in the southeastern highlands of the Algerian desert. They are called the blue people because they grind indigo stones into a fine powder in order to dye their clothes. This powder rubs off on their skin, and the effect is considered quite beautiful.

The Tuareg divide themselves into a class system. They have their own form of nobility and, at the opposite extreme, servants and slaves. Perhaps the most remarkable thing about the Tuareg is that, to some extent, they remain masters of the Sahara, as were their ancestors. In centuries past Tuareg tribesmen were respected for their uncanny skill in guiding caravans through the puzzling desert and maintaining cattle and camel herds in the harsh terrain. Today, the camel-herding tradition of the Tuareg is disappearing.

The fourth Berber group is the Mzab (Mozabites). These people traditionally have occupied the northern fringe of the Sahara Desert, relying on the oases found there for water. Like the Tuareg, the Mzab once were noted guides and traders in the Sahara. In recent generations they have turned to other livelihoods. Some Mzab have even relocated to the northern cities.

Since independence some Algerian educators and artists have focused on renewing the ancient Berber traditions. All but a tiny fraction of Berbers are Muslims today, and yet most still maintain a few religious and social practices that are native to the Maghreb and older than Islam. They honor

A Tuareg man pauses in the Sahara Desert.

certain native saints, for example, and women in Berber communities are somewhat less restricted than are Muslim women in other societies.

The Tuareg are particularly interesting in this regard. In sharp contrast to other Muslim societies, the blue people are matriarchal. In addition, while the women go unveiled, the men cover their faces with the tail end of their turbans. It is believed that evil spirits enter the body through the mouth and nose, so the men cover their faces to keep them out. Women, however, are

Stop signs in Algeria include the English word "Stop," as well as the Arabic equivalents.

believed to be immune to evil spirits because they possess the power of life. Instead, the women wear a headdress. When the weather is harsh, they drape a length of fabric from their dresses over the headdress to create a cool tent over their heads.

One of the ancient traditions of the blue people is a dance called the Guedra. The dance is performed at night around a fire. During the Guedra, the dancer veils herself in the same way that she would to protect from sun and sand, enveloping herself in darkness. During the dance, she will reach and scratch at the darkness, looking for a way to escape. The dance symbolizes the human search for enlightenment. When she is ready, the dancer will fling the veil aside and cast blessings on all the observers. The movements of her hands indicate whom her blessings are for and whether they are for the past, present, or future. The speed and intensity of the Guedra increase over time, and the dance can last until the dancer collapses in a trance.

Of all the dances performed by the blue people, the Guedra is the most important. The Tuareg believe it connects them directly with the spiritual world and protects them from the dangers of their harsh environment.

DAILY LIFE AND SOCIETY

Most Algerians have Arab ancestry and inhabit the cities and towns of the nation's coastal zone. Since independence Algerian leaders have promoted a general Arabization of the country. They have made Arabic the official language and affirmed the values and teachings of Islam. To a great extent, this seems to be a reaction against 130 years of French domination.

As in other Arab countries, firm family structures are important in Algeria. Family loyalty runs deep, and younger Algerians exhibit respect for their elders. Also as in other Arab countries, Algerian women gradually are emerging into a freer lifestyle than in times past, although they are still generally regarded as inferior to men.

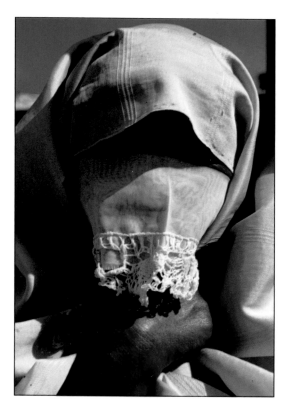

An Algerian woman wears a traditional veil and a white robe called a *haik*. Islamic custom requires that women observe modest dress.

During the long war for independence, some women were engaged in active combat. Afterward, more and more women obtained jobs and enrolled in colleges. Both men and women 18 and older are entitled to vote in Algeria. Still, Muslim traditions remain firm. Most Algerian women veil their faces in public, according to Islamic custom. And Algerian women are still required to have male guardians.

The people of Algeria have followed a variety of religions throughout history. In early times some of the Berbers embraced Carthaginian and, later, Roman gods. After the reign of the Roman Emperor Constantine in the fourth century A.D., Christianity spread widely across North Africa. Then came the Muslims from the east. Today, Islam is the official state religion, and almost all Algerians are of the Malikite sect of Sunni Muslims. Recently, those who follow strict Muslim teachings have increased their influence in the country. A small fraction of the population are Christians; an even smaller fraction are Jews.

Nine years of schooling are required for Algerian children. Education is provided free up through the technical school and university levels. At the time of independence in 1962, fewer than 10 in 100 Algerians could read and write. Today, the literacy rate has risen to about 70 percent. Literacy is higher among men than among women.

Algerians also enjoy better health conditions than the inhabitants of most African countries. Health care, for the most part, is provided free by the government through a national system of health clinics and hospitals. The average life expectancy, about 74 years, is longer today than it was at independence five decades ago. The AIDS virus, which has devastated other parts of Africa, is not a major problem in Algeria. The rate of infant deaths has dropped dramatically, from about 15 percent in 1965 to less than 3 percent today. Serious health concerns in Algeria include lung illnesses such as tuberculosis and pneumonia; stomach disorders; and contagious diseases, including cholera, scarlet fever, venereal diseases, and mumps.

LITERATURE AND MUSIC

Algeria has produced a number of great writers and thinkers. Two of the most famous, Jacques Derrida and Albert Camus, were born in Algeria as the sons of French colonists. Derrida (1930–2004) was a philosopher and critic who is best known for his complex theories known as "deconstruction." This is essentially a method scholars use to read texts in order to understand the meanings and assumptions behind the written words. Camus (1913–1960) was a highly influential author whose works included *The Stranger* (1942); an essay outlining his view of the absurdity of life called *The Myth of Sisyphus* (1942); *The Plague* (1947); and *The Fall* (1956). He received the Nobel Prize for Literature in 1957.

One of the most famous Algerian authors was Mohammed Dib (1920–2003), who wrote more than 30 novels. During the Algerian War for Independence, Dib was expelled from the country by French authorities; many of his later works are set during this period. Dib also published many poems, short stories, and books for children.

Marie-Louise-Taos Amrouche (1913–1976), a woman of Berber ethnicity, is distinguished as the first important female Algerian writer, as well as a Berber activist. Her first novel, the autobiographical *Jacinthe noir,* was published in 1947. In 1966 she helped found the Académie Berbère, an

Algeria's most important living literary figure, writer Assia Djebar (right), speaks with Palestinian author Sahar Kalifa at the 2004 Frankfurt Book Fair in Germany.

organization of Berber artists, writers, and intellectuals. Her older brother, Jean-Elmouhoub Amrouche (1906–1962) is considered one of Algeria's greatest poets.

The most famous living Algerian writer is Fatima-Zohra Imalayen, who writes in French using the pen name Assia Djebar. A strong feminist, most of

Djebar's novels and stories focus on the difficulties faced by women in North African societies. Her novel *Fantasia: An Algerian Cavalcade* (1985) was the first in a series of four novels about women living in the Maghreb. The others include *A Sister to Scheherazade* (1987), *Vast Is the Prison* (1994), and *The White of Algeria* (1996). In 1996 she won the Neustadt Prize for Contributions to World Literature, and in recent years she has been nominated several times for the Nobel Prize. Djebar is generally considered one of North Africa's greatest writers.

Music is also important to the people of Algeria. Raï music is a particular art form developed in western Algeria and brought to the cities by migrants. *Raï* means "the path" or "the way." It can be interpreted as an opinion that is considered wise and true. The old wise men in Algerian culture used to pass on their teachings in the form of poetry. Like many oral traditions, the poems are long and consist not only of sage advice, but a historical record woven with religious implications.

Modern raï music is "rebel" music. Like rap in the United States, modern raï uses heavily suggestive imagery in order to disturb the conservative establishment. The actual music is easy to dance to, borrowing from pop, rock, jazz, and funk. Musicians use any instruments they can acquire in their performances and blend traditional Arabic sounds with Western influences.

Algeria is home to many historical cities. (Opposite) This picture shows the port of Algiers, one of the major economic centers in Algeria. (Right) The minaret of the mosque in Ghardaïa towers above the rest of the city.

6 Cities and Communities

IN AGES PAST Algerian farmers and herders lived in far-flung villages across the coastal zone, in the mountains, and around desert oases. During the French colonial period, administrators created dozens of villages throughout the northern part of the country. Then the long war for independence drastically altered the map of Algeria again. Almost 8,000 communities and villages were destroyed or abandoned. As many as 3 million rural people took refuge in larger towns and cities or were placed in "resettlement" communities. Some of the resettlement locations eventually became new towns.

During the 1970s the Algerian government created several hundred new villages as part of a plan to redistribute the population. Additionally, as in other countries where agriculture is dwindling, rural people have been abandoning their farms, herds, and age-old way of living to seek better conditions in urban areas.

Some of Algeria's seaports and cities date to ancient times. Yet, if the typical foreigner is asked to name a city in Algeria, it's likely only one will come to mind. Algiers is not just the nation's capital; it is one of the most famous cities in the Mediterranean.

ALGIERS

Founded by the Phoenicians, Algiers now covers some 10 miles (16 km) of hilly coastline along the Bay of Algiers. It lies about midway between the country's eastern and western borders. The name "Algiers" means "island" in Arabic. In past centuries the bay indeed contained tiny islands, but most of them have since been leveled or become part of the mainland.

The Carthaginians—and the Romans who fought them—called this important seaport Icosium. Marauding Vandals from Europe in the fifth century A.D. arrived on the North African coast and sacked Icosium. Some 500 years later, Arab-Berber inhabitants made it one of the most powerful centers of trade in the Mediterranean. Later, Algiers came under the control of the Turks, then the French.

The population of Algiers and its suburbs numbers some 17 million—roughly half the country's total population. The city grew at an astonishing rate during the mid-20th century—even during the guerrilla warfare leading up to independence. In that period, foreign oil industry workers and French soldiers joined refugees from tribal mountain villages on the streets. Since then the city has grown steadily.

Algiers has long been a busy international port. During the mid-20th century its harbor became a scene of constant activity. Huge ships brought in tons of building materials—steel, cement, wood—and coal for fuel. Then they filled their holds with Algeria's export *commodities*, mainly farm produce.

ORAN

The city of Oran is a major port and commercial center, located on the Mediterranean coast of northwestern Algeria. Oran was founded in the 10th century by Moorish traders. Today it is the capital of the Oran *wilaya*, with a population of about 700,000.

At the time Algeria became independent, many Europeans lived in Oran. However, in July 1962 Algerian nationalists massacred some 3,000 unarmed Europeans living in the city. Most of the Europeans in Oran—more than 200,000 people—soon left the country. It took years for Oran to recover.

The great writer Albert Camus was born in Oran, and used the city as a setting for two of his greatest novels, *The Plague* and *The Stranger*. French fashion designer Yves Saint Laurent was also born in Oran, as were the influential Raï musicians Cheb Khaled and Rachid Taha.

SIDI BEL ABBÈS

Inland Algerian cities and towns have grown and developed for different reasons. Sidi Bel Abbès in northwestern Algeria originally was a French Foreign Legion post, built by legionnaires in 1847. Until independence more than a century later, it continued to be a principal training center for the military. Sidi Bel Abbès is now home to an estimated 200,000 people. It is located near the seasonal river of Wadi Mekerra, and local industry includes agriculture and farm machinery manufacturing.

GHARDAÏA

Ghardaïa is located in the Mzab Valley, which is listed by the UN as a World Heritage Site. There are five cities in the valley inhabited by the Mozabites. The people are considered Islamic puritans and maintain stark houses and strict dress. Ghardaïa has hotels and restaurants to serve tourists, while the smaller towns do not allow outsiders to stay the night. Mozabite towns exhibit advanced urban planning. Each was split into a *ksar* (winter town), *wahat* (summer town), and cemetery in the desert. Winter towns such as Ghardaïa have a mosque, a Friday mosque, a residential area, an open market, and fortifications. The houses center around a shaded courtyard and provide rooftop terraces to enjoy the open air.

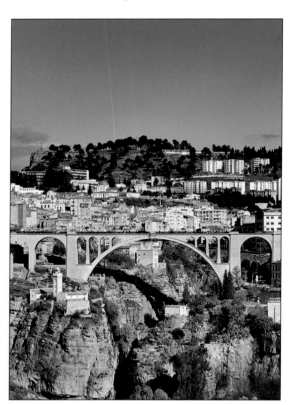

Scenic Constantine is the third-largest city in Algeria.

TLEMCEN

Tlemcen is the capital of a province in northwestern Algeria with the same name. It is home to 180,000 people. The city, which was once the center of a Berber empire, was captured by the Ottomans in 1553. The cool mountain climate has made Tlemcen a popular tourist destination for centuries. Tlemcen is home to olive plantations and vineyards and is also known for textiles and crafts. One of the major sites to visit is the Tomb of Sidi Bou Mediene, a religious leader who lived there. The tomb of Algeria's second president, Houari Boumédiènne, is also located in Tlemcen.

CONSTANTINE

At the eastern end of the Tell, the city of Constantine became prominent in Phoenician times because of its "natural fortress" location atop a rugged plateau. It originally was known as Cirta, based on the word for "city" in Phoenician. The walls constructed by the Romans still stand, and the city is so well protected that the Vandals failed to capture it when they overran the region during the fifth century. French forces in the 1830s captured it only after two bloody attempts, taking disastrous losses in doing so. During World War II Constantine served as a base of command for Allied forces in northern Africa.

Constantine is one of the country's most interesting cities. Its history of more than 2,000 years is preserved in its architecture. Elements of Roman, Islamic, 19th-century French, and modern designs are plainly seen.

TAMANRASSET

South of the Tell zone, most of the few inhabitants live around oases. The only sizeable town is Tamanrasset, located in the Ahaggar Highlands of the southeast, near Mount Tahat. To the south is the Sahara Desert. Tamanrasset is the chief city of the Tuareg.

A CALENDAR OF ALGERIAN FESTIVALS

As in other Middle Eastern and African societies, most of the celebrations in Algeria are related to religious, family, or tribal events. Weddings and harvest gatherings, for example, are times for local merrymaking. Traditional dancing, music, and food usually are key ingredients.

Muslim Holidays

Muslim holidays coincide with the lunar calendar, which is shorter than the solar calendar familiar to Westerners. That means Islamic holy months and days do not occur in the same Western calendar months from year to year.

The **Muslim New Year** marks the beginning of the Islamic month known as Muharram.

Mawlid an-Nabi, the commemoration of the birthday of the Prophet Mohammed, is celebrated by prayer and often a procession to the local mosque. Families gather for feasts, often featuring the foods that were reportedly the favorites of Mohammed: dates, grapes, almonds, and honey. This holiday occurs on the 12th of Rabi'-ul-Awwal.

The month of **Ramadan** is perhaps the best-known Islamic calendar event.

During Ramadan, Muslims are supposed to fast during the day, pray, and perform deeds of kindness for the poor. At the end of Ramadan comes **Eid al-Fitr**, a feast and celebration lasting three days. During Eid al-Fitr, schools and businesses close. People put on new clothing and exchange presents.

Eid al-Adha is a special occasion on which Muslims reflect on Abraham's ancient offer to sacrifice his son Isaac to God. Eid al-Adha occurs at the end of the *hajj*, the annual pilgrimage to Mecca. Muslims who cannot travel to Mecca observe Eid al-Adha at home.

January

New Year's Day is observed in Algeria like it is observed in most of the world.

May

Labor Day is also observed in Algeria like it is in most of the world.

June

Commemoration Day on June 19 celebrates the day Colonel Houari Boumédiènne came to power. He is remembered for having brought access to healthcare and education to his people.

July

Independence Day is July 5. This marks the day that Algerians gained independence from France in 1962.

November

November 1 is celebrated as **Revolution Day**. It marks the beginning of the long fight for independence from France, which began on November 1, 1954.

RECIPES

L'Ham el Hlou (Lamb)

1 lb. lamb
1/2 lb. dry prunes
1/4 lb. raisins
1 onion
1 tbs. cinnamon
Dash of salt
1/2 cup oil or butter
1 cup sugar

Directions:
1. Soak prunes and raisins in water 15-20 minutes.
2. Cut lamb into small chunks and onion into bits.
3. Brown lamb, onion, cinnamon, salt, and oil (butter). Add water and bring mixture to a boil. Add prunes, raisins, and sugar.
4. Cover and simmer approximately 20 minutes or until lamb is tender and prunes are inflated. Uncover to reduce sauce.

Notes: Beef may be substituted for lamb. If available, a tablespoon of *mzhar* (orange blossom water) may be added along with the prunes, raisins, and sugar.

Chicken Shorba (Soup)

1 1/2 lbs. cubed chicken
1 grated yellow onion
1/2 small, grated potato
1/2 grated zucchini
1 halved carrot
1/2 halved rib celery
1/4 cup dried chickpeas, soaked overnight in water, then drained (canned chickpeas may be substituted)
2 tsp. salt
1/2 tsp. black pepper
1/2 tsp. cinnamon
1 tbs. paprika
2 tbs. tomato paste
1 tbs. olive oil
8 cups water
1/2 cup orzo or other type of soup pasta
1 tbs. chopped parsley
1 tsp. chopped fresh mint leaves
Slices of lemon

Directions:
1. Put half a cup of water in a large pot along with chicken, onion, grated potato, zucchini, carrot, celery, salt, pepper, cinnamon, paprika, tomato paste, and oil. If using dried chickpeas, include them here.
2. Cover and sauté over low heat for 20 minutes.
3. Add remaining water. Bring to a boil and simmer 45 minutes. Add pasta. If using canned chickpeas, include them now. Cook 10 minutes. Add parsley and mint and serve with lemon slices.

Couscous

2 lbs. cubed chicken breast
1 tbs. butter
1 tbs. olive oil
1 sliced medium onion
1 chopped large tomato
1 stick cinnamon
1 package couscous
1 can chickpeas
Salt and pepper to taste

Directions:
1. Sauté all ingredients except couscous and chick-peas until meat is done.
2. Add chickpeas.
3. Simmer. Mix with couscous and serve.

Chlada Fakya (Fruit Salad)

1/4 cubed melon
2 cubed apples
2 sliced bananas
5 peeled/seeded/chopped oranges
3/4 cup orange juice
1/4 cup lemon juice
2 tbs. sugar
1 tsp. vanilla
1/2 tsp. cinnamon

Directions:
1. Mix all ingredients and chill.

Coclo (Meatballs)

1 lb. ground beef
1/2 cup rice
1 bulb finely chopped garlic
1 beaten medium egg
1/2 tsp. salt
1/4 tsp. pepper
1/2 tsp. ground bay leaf
1/8 tsp. ground mace
1/8 tsp. thyme
2 tbs. olive oil
1 finely chopped medium onion
1/2 bunch cilantro, bundle-tied
3/4 cup water

Directions:
1. Mix beef, rice, garlic, egg, salt, pepper, bay leaf, mace, thyme, and oil. Shape into two big meatballs.
2. Put onion, cilantro, and water in a pan, add meatballs, and cover. Simmer two hours or slightly longer over low heat.
3. Dispose of cilantro. Serve with rice or couscous.

GLOSSARY

amnesty—a pardon granted by a government for acts committed by members of a group of people.

colons—European settlers in Algeria; also called pieds-noirs.

commodities—items of trade, such as farm products and minerals, that can be exported in large quantities to other countries.

corsairs—Islamic sea raiders of the Mediterranean.

emir—the title of a ruler in an Islamic country.

export—to sell goods to foreign countries.

hydrocarbons—raw products that include fuel sources such as petroleum.

import—to buy goods from foreign countries.

Islamist—a person who believes Islamic laws and restrictions should be the basis for a nation's political system. Islamists generally insist on strict adherence to religious teachings.

jamaa—a council of men in a Kabyle (Berber) village.

Maghreb—a name for the coastal region of Africa's northwestern Mediterranean coast, which includes all of coastal Algeria and parts of Libya and Morocco.

oasis—a rare place in a desert where a permanent water supply supports plant life.

parallel—extending alongside a line or object, rather than intersecting with it.

pieds-noirs—European settlers in Algeria; also called colons.

savanna—a grassy landscape with scattered trees and shrubs.

sirocco—a choking summer wind that frequently blows into countries around the Sahara Desert.

socialist—pertaining to a political system in which businesses, industries, and farms are owned collectively by all the citizens of a country and controlled by the government; it is a basis for communistic forms of government.

theocracy—a government in which religious leaders make laws and rule based on their perception of what a divine being (such as God or Allah) wishes.

tribute—a payment by one government to another, acknowledging submission or as the price for protection.

utility—a basic service required for living, such as a water or transportation system.

wilaya—a governmental province in Algeria.

PROJECT AND REPORT IDEAS

Cave Art

Examine pictures of the ancient cave paintings discovered in the Tassili-n-Ajjer highlands of Algeria. Write a paper interpreting what you think the people are doing and what types of animals are in the picture. What materials might the artists have used for the paintings? Why do you think the pictures were painted? How do you think they have lasted for so many centuries? On a rough surface, using crude coloring materials, make a drawing that could show future generations what you would like for them to know about your world today.

Conquer the Great Sahara Desert

Identify the main cities of nations to the south, southeast, and southwest of Algeria. Map a network of roads through the desert connecting northern Algeria's inhabited zone with those destinations. You must circumvent rugged highland areas and, to the extent possible, take advantage of oases that are indicated on maps.

Desert Facts

Research the Sahara Desert and its plant and animal life. Write a true-false quiz with which to test your classmates' (or your teacher's) knowledge about the desert and perhaps amaze them with curious facts. Sample questions: "Panthers are known to roam the Sahara (T-F)." "The Sahara is the largest desert on earth (T-F)." "The Sahara once flourished with plant and animal life (T-F)." "Mountains are found in parts of the Sahara (T-F)." "Temperatures sometimes drop to freezing in the Sahara (T-F)."

PROJECT AND REPORT IDEAS

Critique the Algerian National Anthem

Listen carefully to the score of the national anthem (recordings can be found in multimedia encyclopedias or online). Do parts of it remind you of famous European classical works or American popular works? Which ones? Why?

Algeria's Most Famous Pirate

Study the legacy of Kheir-ed-din Barbarossa, the famous corsair leader who drove the Spaniards from their island fortress in the Bay of Algiers. What effects did Barbarossa have on Algerian history?

Improve Algeria's Economic Outlook

You have been placed in charge of economic improvement for the government. Your great challenge is to find new sources of income apart from the sale of oil and gas. Your country's natural resources appear to be quite limited. What can be done? Can you build a tourism industry? What would be the major attractions you would promote? Is there potential in expanding your coastal fishing industry? How can farming be improved?

CHRONOLOGY

Prehistoric times: Primitive cultures inhabit the fertile area that now is the Sahara Desert.

9th to 6th centuries B.C.: Carthage becomes a powerful city dominating coastal North Africa.

264–146 B.C.: Punic Wars fought between Carthage and Rome. Rome ultimately wins control of northern Africa.

A.D. 429: Vandals crossing from Spain invade northern Africa in the declining years of the Roman Empire.

7th and 8th centuries: Arabs spread across North Africa from the Middle East, intermarry with native Berbers, and begin to dominate the region.

11th century: Large numbers of Moors flee Spain and settle in North Africa.

16th century: Ottoman Turks gain control over the Maghreb region.

1529: Kheir-ed-din Barbarossa, a corsair captain, takes over Algiers and drives the Spanish garrison from its fort on the island of Peñon in the Bay of Algiers. Barbarossa brings the Barbary Coast into the Ottoman Empire.

1830: In combating the infamous Barbary pirates of the lower Mediterranean coast, French forces take control of Algiers.

1954: Beginning of the war for Algerian independence from France.

1960: The United Nations votes to recognize Algeria's right of self-government.

1962: A cease-fire is arranged between French forces and Algerian FLN revolutionaries. Algeria becomes an independent nation; hundreds of thousands of pieds-noirs, French nationals who have been living in the country, flee en masse; Ahmad Ben Bella becomes Algeria's first premier.

1965: Colonel Houari Boumédiènne becomes president after leading an army coup to overthrow Ben Bella.

1978: President Boumédiènne dies and is succeeded in office by Chadli Bendjedid.

1988: A new constitution opens the way for a multiple-party political system.

1991: The Islamic Salvation Front (FIS) wins national elections and appears ready to gain control of Algeria's legislature.

1992: The Algerian military forces president Bendjedid to resign, takes control of the government, and cancels elections. In response, the FIS and other Islamist groups begin a civil war against the government.

1999: Abdelaziz Bouteflika becomes president.

2000: The militant Islamic Salvation Army is disbanded; many of its members are granted amnesty by the government.

2002: The National Liberation Front (FLN) wins the majority of seats in elections to the National People's Assembly. Tamazight is recognized as a national language.

2004: Abdelaziz Bouteflika is reelected president in a landslide.

2006: Russia forgives $4.74 billion in Algerian debt in exchange for a $7.5 billion weapons contract with Russian arms dealers.

2007: All-African Games held in Algiers; Multiple bombings by al-Qaeda-affiliated terrorists.

2008: Terrorist bombings continue. National Assembly lifts presidential term limits.

2009: Abdelaziz Bouteflika is re-elected for a third time. Nigeria, Niger, and Algeria agree to jointly build a major oil pipeline.

2010: Algeria, Mauritania, Mali, and Niger officially join forces to fight terrorism.

2011: Protests against the government erupt throughout Algeria, with demonstrators demanding democracy and greater economic opportunities.

2012: In legislative elections, pro-government parties win a majority of seats, leading Islamists to complain that the election was unfair.

Le Sueur, James. D. *Algeria Since 1989: Between Terror and Democracy*. London: Zed, 2010

McDougall, James. *History and the Culture of Nationalism in Algeria*. New York: Cambridge University Press, 2006.

Morrow, James. *Algeria*. Philadelphia: Mason Crest Publishers, 2009.

Phillips, John, and Evans, Martin. *Algeria: Anger of the Dispossessed*. New Haven: Yale University Press, 2008.

Ruedy, John. *Modern Algeria: The Origins and Development of a Nation*. 2nd ed. Bloomington: Indiana University Press, 2005.

Economic and Political Information

http://news.bbc.co.uk/2/hi/middle_east/811140.stm
http://algiers.usembassy.gov/
https://www.cia.gov/library/publications/the-world-factbook/geos/ag.html

Culture and Festivals

http://www.everyculture.com/A-Bo/Algeria.html
http://www.algeria.com/culture/
http://www.kwintessential.co.uk/resources/global-etiquette/algeria.html

History and Geography

http://www.africa.com/algeria
http://africanhistory.about.com/od/algeria/Algeria.htm
http://kids.yahoo.com/reference/encyclopedia/entry?id=Algeria
http://www.factmonster.com/ipka/A0107272.html

Travel Information

http://www.lonelyplanet.com/algeria
http://travel.state.gov/travel/cis_pa_tw/cis/cis_1087.html
http://www.world66.com/africa/algeria

Embassy of the People's Democratic Republic of Algeria
2118 Kalorama Rd., NW
Washington, DC 20008
Tel: (202) 265-2800
Fax: (202) 667-2174
Email: mail@algeria-us.org
Website: http://www.algeria-us.org

The Permanent Mission of Algeria to the United Nations
326 E 48th St.
New York, NY 10017-1747
Tel: (212) 750-1960
Fax: (212) 759-5274
E-mail: mission@algeria-un.org
Website: http://www.algeria-un.org

U.S. Embassy in Algeria
05 Chemin Cheikh Bachir Ibrahimi
El-Biar 16030
Alger Algerie
Tel: 0770-08-2000
Fax: 021-60-7335
Email: Algiers_webmaster@state.gov
Website: http://algiers.usembassy.gov

U.S. Department of State
Bureau of Consular Affairs
2100 Pennsylvania Ave. NW, 4th Floor
Washington, DC 20037
Tel: (202) 736 9130

INDEX

Numbers in **bold italic** refer to captions.

CONTRIBUTORS/PICTURE CREDITS

Professor Robert I. Rotberg is Director of the Program on Intrastate Conflict and Conflict Resolution at the Kennedy School, Harvard University, and President of the World Peace Foundation. He is the author of a number of books and articles on Africa, including *A Political History of Tropical Africa* and *Ending Autocracy, Enabling Democracy: The Tribulations of Southern Africa*.

Daniel E. Harmon is an author and editor in Spartanburg, South Carolina. He has written more than 50 nonfiction books, one historical mystery short story collection, and numerous magazine and newspaper articles. Harmon has served for many years as associate editor of *Sandlapper: The Magazine of South Carolina* and as editor of *The Lawyer's PC*, a national computer newsletter. His special interests include world history and folk music.